Faith *over* Fear

ALSO BY MATT RAWLE

The Faith of a Mockingbird

The Redemption of Scrooge

What Makes a Hero?

The Gift of the Nutcracker

The Grace of Les Miserables

The Heart That Grew Three Sizes

Jesus Revealed

Experiencing Christmas

The Final Days

**With Magrey R. deVega,
Ingrid McIntyre, and April Casperson**

Almost Christmas

FOR MORE
INFORMATION, VISIT
MATTRAWLE.COM

MATT RAWLE

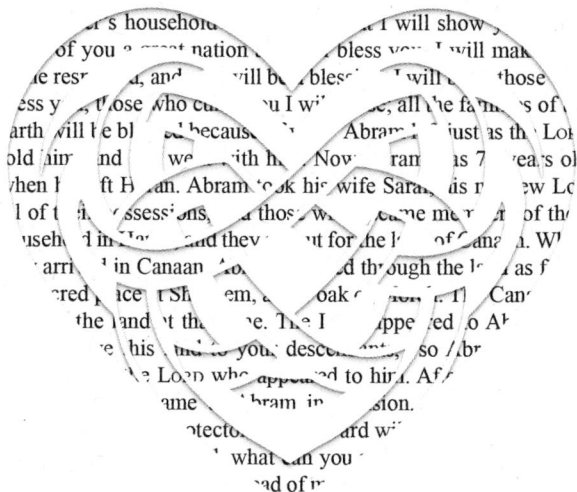

Faith *over* Fear

Abraham's Imperfect Journey

Abingdon Press | Nashville

Faith *over* **Fear**
Abraham's Imperfect Journey

Copyright © 2025 Abingdon Press
All rights reserved.

Library of Congress Control Number: 2025932880
978-1-7910-3939-4

MANUFACTURED IN THE
UNITED STATES OF AMERICA

CONTENTS

Download a
FREE Discussion Guide for
Faith *over* Fear.

MATT RAWLE

Faith *over* Fear

Abraham's Imperfect Journey

Scan the QR code
on the right or visit
**https://formtitan.com
/s/w2oh**
to download.

INTRODUCTION

Faith is not a straight line. It twists and turns, sometimes doubling back on itself in ways we never expect. It is not a formula, nor is it a guarantee of smooth sailing. It is a journey marked by doubt and discovery, by moments of bold trust and hesitant obedience. It is, in many ways, an imperfect pursuit. And perhaps no figure in Scripture embodies this paradox more than Abraham.

We often speak of Abraham as a hero of faith, the man who, without question, left his homeland at God's command, the one whose trust in the divine promise made him the father of many nations. But when we slow down and take a closer look at his story, we see something far more complicated. Abraham is not simply the faithful patriarch who gets everything right. He is also the man who hedges his bets, who takes matters into his own hands when God's timing doesn't align with his expectations. He is the man who fears for his own life and places his wife in compromising situations to protect himself. He is the man who laughs at

God's promises and then, at the very last moment, is forced to wrestle with what it means to trust God even when the cost seems unbearable.

To understand Abraham's journey, we need to embrace the faithful assumption that God is always calling us forward—to traverse new territory. This is not simply about packing up and moving to a new place, as Abraham did, but about an openness of spirit, a willingness to step beyond what is known and familiar. Faith is, at its core, the ability to trust in a promise not yet fulfilled, to say yes to something uncertain, to take the next step even when we cannot see the full path ahead. But before we can move forward with conviction, we must take stock of where we are. Knowing our location—both physically and spiritually—is essential, because without that awareness, we risk mistaking motion for progress. Abraham did not wander aimlessly; he moved with purpose, even when the destination remained unclear. His journey reminds us that faith does not eliminate uncertainty; it teaches us how to walk through it.

These days, it feels as though we are navigating a world with no reliable playbook. The pace of change is relentless, and every day seems to introduce a new precedent, a fresh challenge, a shift we did not anticipate, rife with ambient confusion. Anxiety has become so pervasive it feels like the very air we breathe. In my work with the Hub4Innovation, a platform for churches to explore and discuss new ideas, I have had the privilege of interviewing church leaders from across the country, and *anxiety* is the most common word that keeps surfacing to describe the current moment in ministry. It's the unsettling feeling of holding a map that has served us well up to this point, only to realize that the road ahead is missing from it. The path once drawn with confidence now dissolves into blank space, leaving us grasping for clarity. But perhaps this is precisely where faith becomes most real—not in the certainty of well-marked trails but in the courage to step forward despite the unknown. Maybe this is where we, like Abraham, learn that faith is not about having all the answers but about trusting that our questions are better today than they were yesterday.

We are being called to walk off the map, so to speak. What does it mean to follow a God who calls us into the unknown? First, I think it means recognizing that yes and no occupy the same place at the same time. A yes to something is always a no to something else. I think many of our decisions about what to do, how to act, and how to engage are simplified when we realize that decisions never happen in a vacuum. When I say yes to an evening meeting, I'm saying no to helping my children with homework. When I say yes to sabbath rest, I am saying no to being defined by the work I produce. A yes to movement is a no to stagnation, and so on. In lieu of diving into a much more complicated ethical discussion of means and ends, for now, to better understand Abraham's story and ours, it will be important to keep in mind that yes and no always exist concurrently.

Stepping into new territory always involves loss. When my sister began seriously dating her future husband, I felt this loss keenly. Our family had always been close, and now there was someone new—someone I hadn't chosen—who was suddenly part of our gatherings, our traditions, our time together. What made it seemingly worse at the time was that he seemed to be good at everything. Confession: I called him "Mr. Perfect." One year for Christmas, I got my mother an album of bagpipe music that I really wanted for myself. Mr. Perfect made her a new mailbox out of oak in his workshop. And so the pattern continued.

I love my now brother-in-law. He is an amazing husband, father, teacher, and administrator, among other things, though when I was younger, I remember feeling that something was shifting, even as I knew it was good. Loss is often like that. It is the necessary cost of growth. Abraham had to leave his home, his land, his family to follow God's call. Later, he would even have to lay Isaac on the altar, offering up the very thing he had waited for, trusting that God's promise did not end with his own understanding. Every act of faith involves a letting go, a willingness to release what is familiar to embrace what God is doing next.

When Abraham said yes to God's call, he simultaneously said no to everything that had once defined his security—his homeland, his extended family, the stability of a life he had always known. There were no road maps, no assurances of success, no fine print detailing what was ahead. There was only the promise that God would go with him. And yet, like all of us, he wrestled with the weight of that promise. It is one thing to believe in God's faithfulness in theory, another to trust it when everything feels uncertain. When the path is unclear, we are often tempted to force clarity, to take matters into our own hands, to manufacture what only God can provide. We mistake divine favor for something we must capture, control, or protect.

Faith is not about securing God's promises through diligence or effort—it is about leaning in to the mystery of them. When we try to orchestrate the outcomes ourselves, we either cling too tightly to what feels safe or rush ahead and break things open before their time. Abraham did both. Yet this is the very heart of faith—not the absence of fear but the courage to walk forward despite it. To trust that even in our stumbles, our doubts, our failed attempts at control, God's promises remain unshaken. Abraham's story reminds us that faith is not about arriving at certainty; it is about remaining in conversation with God. It is about taking the next step even when the way is obscured, about leaning in to trust when every impulse tells us to turn back.

Abraham's journey is not one of pristine, unshakable faith, and neither is ours. We falter, we question, and we have moments when fear speaks louder than faith. But God's promises are not contingent on our consistency. The call of faith is not to never struggle but to keep walking, even when we are unsure, knowing that grace is always ahead of us, drawing us forward.

Fear is woven into the fabric of the human experience. It is primal, instinctual, and often deeply rational. Fear is what keeps us from stepping off a cliff's edge. It is what makes us hesitate before leaping into the unknown. But faith, by its very nature, calls us into places that fear warns us to avoid. Faith asks us to step into the uncertain, to trust what we cannot see, to hold all things loosely.

This story matters because today there is much to fear. It seems every day there is another troubling news story fraught with confusion and leading to disdain for our neighbor. As a white, Southern, male preacher, it stings for me to say, "Don't be afraid." On the list of "First they came for the . . ." I'm at the bottom. With that said, Abraham's journey is our journey. His fears mirror our own—the fear of the unknown, the fear of scarcity, the fear that God's promises will not come to pass. His missteps are all too familiar—the times we take control rather than trust, the times we prioritize safety over obedience, the times we let fear dictate our choices. And yet, through it all, God remains present. God does not abandon Abraham to his fear, and God does not abandon us to ours.

This tension—between faith and fear—is the defining struggle of Abraham's life. When God calls Abraham in Genesis 12, the directive is startlingly vague: "Go from your country and your kindred and your father's house to the land I will show you" (v. 1). There are no coordinates, no clear destination, no assurance beyond the promise that God will bless him. And remarkably, Abraham goes. He leaves behind everything familiar and steps into an undefined future. At this moment, it seems as though fear has no hold on him. But as the story unfolds, we see that this is not entirely true.

Only a few verses later, when famine forces Abraham to seek refuge in Egypt, we see the first crack in his certainty. Fear creeps in. He worries that the Egyptians will see Sarah's beauty and kill him to take her as their own. So rather than trust in the God who called him, he devises his own plan: he tells Sarah to say she is his sister. It is a half-truth but a whole betrayal. His fear leads him to self-preservation at the cost of integrity, at the cost of trust. And yet, God does not abandon him. This does not mean God approves of this deception or condones the abuse that Sarah must have endured. Interestingly, after this episode in Egypt, God begins to incorporate Sarah into the promise that seemed to have been only offered to Abraham's ears. Maybe this is God's way of remaining faithful to the promise but pivoting away from Abraham's lack of integrity.

Introduction

Fear has a way of distorting vision, of making what was once clear seem uncertain and unreliable. Abraham, who once set out with bold trust in God's promise, now finds himself grasping for control, seeking security through deception and human strategy rather than divine faithfulness. His decision in Egypt was driven by fear—fear of death, fear of the unknown, fear that perhaps God would not protect him after all. And though God remains faithful, the consequences of Abraham's choices ripple outward, affecting not just his own journey but Sarah's as well.

But fear is not easily silenced. Even after witnessing God's provision, even after experiencing divine rescue, Abraham and Sarah still wrestle with the unbearable weight of waiting. The years stretch long, and the promise feels increasingly distant. What began as faith now strains under the pressure of delay. And so, in an attempt to force fulfillment, they take action—turning to their own solutions, their own understanding.

God makes a promise that Abraham will have descendants as numerous as the stars. But years pass, and no child is born. Doubt takes root. Sarah, too, grows impatient. The weight of waiting bends their faith, stretching it thin. They decide to take matters into their own hands. Sarah gives her servant Hagar to Abraham, and together they conceive a child, Ishmael. This act of improvisation, of human control grasping for divine promise, leads only to tension and brokenness. What was meant as a solution creates deeper wounds—jealousy festers, resentment takes hold, and soon Hagar is cast out into the wilderness, bearing both the weight of rejection and the fragile hope of her son's future.

In this moment, we see not only Abraham and Sarah's impatience but also the cost of trying to force what only God can give. The promise had been spoken, but the waiting had become unbearable. How often do we find ourselves in the same place? When prayers seem to go unanswered, when God's timing does not align with our own, we, too, grasp for control, convincing ourselves that a shortcut is better than uncertainty. But like Abraham and Sarah, our attempts to manufacture resolution often create more complications than clarity. Their decision—born from frustration rather than faith—does not just impact them; it disrupts the lives of those around them. Hagar is drawn into a story she never chose, and Ishmael, though beloved by God, becomes a symbol of the fractures that impatience can create.

The God who saw Abraham's fear in Egypt also sees Hagar's tears in the wilderness. When she flees, God meets her there, offering not only survival but a promise of her own—a future for Ishmael, a reminder that God's faithfulness extends beyond human failure. It is a stunning moment in Scripture, one that reminds us that God's promises are not held hostage by our mistakes.

Old wounds do not heal overnight. The fractures between Hagar and Sarah, between Ishmael and Isaac, do not disappear simply because God's plan moves forward. This, too, is part of faith's complexity: the realization that God's faithfulness does not erase the consequences of our choices but works through them, redeeming even what is broken.

God's promise still stands, despite desperation. The covenant was never dependent on their perfect faithfulness but on God's unwavering grace. We are conditioned to think of faith as something we either have or do not have, as a binary between belief and doubt. But Abraham's story suggests otherwise. Faith is not a single decision but a continual process. It is not a mountain we conquer but a path we walk. Sometimes we move forward boldly. Other times we stumble and hesitate. And sometimes we double back, wondering if we heard God correctly at all.

What makes Abraham's story so compelling is that his faith is neither perfect nor static. It is a dynamic, evolving relationship with God. He questions. He bargains. He falters. And yet, he keeps moving forward. He keeps showing up. And God keeps showing up for him.

This book is an invitation to wrestle with faith in the same way Abraham did—not as a pristine ideal but as a messy, complicated, and deeply human endeavor. It is an invitation to acknowledge our fears without letting them define us, to embrace the imperfections in our journey while trusting in the perfect faithfulness of God. It is a reminder that faith and fear are not mutually exclusive, but that faith, even an imperfect faith, is still enough.

God does not demand perfection—only that we trust enough to take the next step. And maybe that is the good news buried in Abraham's imperfect journey: That faith, even when it stumbles, is still faith. That obedience, even when hesitant, still moves us forward. And that God's promises, even when we doubt them, remain steadfast. Perhaps you have felt the same pull that Abraham did—the invitation to step into the unknown, to leave behind the comfortable in pursuit of something greater. Perhaps you have also wrestled with moments of doubt, of wondering if you misheard God, or it may seem that everyone you know is mishearing what God is saying.

Abraham's life reminds us that faith is not about having it all figured out but moving even when the path ahead is unclear. It is about holding on to hope, even when God's promises seem distant. It is about believing that the journey itself—the steps, the missteps, the stumbles and recoveries—is part of something greater. Faith over fear. It is a choice we make daily, a posture of trust that says, *Even when I am afraid, I will follow. Even when I doubt, I will take the next step. Even when I falter, I believe that God is leading me forward.*

Faith is rarely enough on its own. It always needs help—help from community, help from ancestors, traditions, and memory, help from the grace of a God who sees us even when we are too afraid to see ourselves. Abraham's journey is a testament to this. He did not walk alone. He was surrounded by people who influenced his choices—some for better, some for worse. His faith was shaped in conversation, refined in relationship. When his belief wavered, God did not rebuke him. Instead, God showed up in the form of new assurances, unexpected encounters, and relentless patience.

What if faith is not about mustering strength but about recognizing our dependence? What if it is less about certainty and more about the courage to keep asking for help? To keep looking for God in the voices around us, in the questions that stretch us, in the moments that remind us we were never meant to do this alone?

Abraham's story is unfinished, and so is ours. The road ahead is unmarked, full of twists we cannot yet see. So where do we go from here? And more important, who will walk with us? Let's walk this road together. Let's explore Abraham's imperfect journey and find within it a reflection of our own. Let's trust that the God who called him is calling us still—leading us, shaping us, and walking with us, every step of the way.

CHAPTER 1
FAITH OVER COMFORT

This past Thanksgiving—or what we fondly call the Grand South Louisiana Holiday Tour—we had just enough time to visit my father-in-law's hunting camp north of Baton Rouge. It's the sort of place where time stretches, where memories linger in the air like the heavy Southern humidity. We hadn't been to the camp in more than twenty years. Obviously unrelated, our last visit happened to coincide with the first and only time I ever helped slaughter a deer. Needless to say, I hadn't been in a rush to return. Yet there we were, two decades later, navigating the familiar curves of the old road, squeezing past the orange cones marking the edge of the driveway and ditch. The past folded over the present, and for a moment, it was like we had never left.

The hunting camp looked like I had remembered, even though there was a newer shelter built next door to the previous one, which remained untouched since a flood several years ago ravaged the interior. It's the kind of place where the trees stand watch and where time forgets to hurry. It struck me, standing in the crunch of gravel, how much of life is defined by places that stay with us. Places that hold something of who we are, or perhaps where we leave pieces of ourselves behind. The longer we stood there, the more I realized how comforting the familiar can be. There is an allure to it—a safety in what we know, a security in what's predictable.

But accompanying the comfort of familiarity was a quiet tug that made me feel that staying in familiar places can sometimes keep us from moving forward. It's like the pull of an anchor: steady and secure, but ultimately immovable. We all have those anchors in our lives—places, people, routines— that whisper to us, *Stay here, it's safer this way.* And while safety and familiarity have their place, they can become the very things that hold us back when God is calling us to step into something new. In that moment, I thought about the tension we all feel: the desire for comfort versus the call to courage. It's a tension as old as time, and it's a tension that requires great faith.

But here's the thing about faith: comfort and predictability rarely have a seat at the table. What happens when

God calls us away from the familiar? When we must leave the places we've built our lives around, either because of calling or necessity, opportunity or heartbreak? What does it mean to leave well—to step forward when the future feels uncertain, when the unknown stretches out like a blank canvas? It's easy to praise God from the safety of the shore, but faith often asks us to wade into deeper waters, into the places where our feet no longer touch solid ground. Faith over comfort. Faith over fear.

Take Abraham,[1] for example. Abraham, the father of Judaism, Christianity, and Islam—a man who is often made to be the pinnacle of faithfulness. But Abraham's story isn't as clean-cut as we make it out to be. It is a story riddled with doubt, hesitation, and missteps. In Genesis, when God calls Abraham to leave his home, the command is strikingly clear: "Go from your country and your kindred, and your father's house to the land that I will show you" (Genesis 12:1). God didn't give him a map. There were no markers, no guarantees. It wasn't just about leaving his home; it was about leaving his comfort. He was called to leave his assumptions of what life should look like, his certainty about how his story should end, and his very identity, which was tied to his familial land.

---

[1] For the sake of simplicity, instead of bouncing back and forth between "Abram" and "Abraham," I'm going to exclusively use "Abraham." I will also do likewise with "Sarah."

Imagine this for a moment. God doesn't just ask Abraham to relocate; God asks him to redefine his entire life. God doesn't promise Abraham comfort. Comfort is an easy thing to worship, isn't it? It wraps itself around us like a warm blanket, whispering, *Stay here. You've earned it. You deserve it.* I've called this phenomenon "nostalgic scarcity." It's the temptation to use our limited resources to recapture the past. I'm not so trite to suggest that we can't recapture the past. We might craft experiences that do offer a beautiful sense of the comfort of childhood memories, of when, we assume, things were simpler. As I get older, I am nearly overwhelmed with the "warm blanket of happiness" when I see the original Nintendo Entertainment System or hear a favorite song from the mid-eighties, so I understand the feeling and temptation of reliving happy times. But faith asks something more. Faith calls us to step outside the blanket fort, to trust in God's provision more than our own plans.

I know this is true because I see it everywhere—in Scripture, in life, in my own predictable routines. Every morning, I meticulously map out my to-do list. I prioritize tasks, set reminders, and use apps to hold myself accountable. I am very comfortable with improvisation, but I also crave order. Order makes improvisation possible. I want my days to be manageable, particularly in a world where absurdity seems to outpace even the sharpest satire. Did I read that headline right? What did the school board decide? What wild thing did that politician just say? There's a part of me that longs for stillness, for the comfort of a quieter world. And yet, as I dive deeper into God's story, I'm reminded again and again that comfort can turn into complacency. "Be still and know that I am God" doesn't mean to be stagnant.

We see this tension in Scripture, don't we? The garden of Eden was a place of provision for both body and soul. Humanity had what it needed for nourishment as well as companionship with God. I used to imagine that the garden of Eden was a set place with definitive boundaries, like having some kind of archway reading "Welcome to the Garden of Eden," denoting what was in the garden and what was outside. Now, I'm not so sure. What makes more sense to me is that the garden was wherever humanity and God communed. Tilling the garden is less about cultivating crops than it is intentionality with the divine. At least, it seems that later in the story, the necessity of farming is no blessing.

The garden wasn't perfect. It wasn't even good. God's proclamation of goodness upon creation is unique to Genesis 1. The divine's first words in the second creation account are riddled with qualified abundance and absence. The human can freely eat, save one tree. God looks upon the human and says that it is "not good" for the human to be alone. Before there was sin, there was scarcity, and this scarcity breeds fear.

Adam and Eve ate from the tree of the knowledge of good and evil because they feared scarcity. They feared that what God had provided wasn't enough, or they didn't trust that the tree should be left alone. Interesting, God, too, responds in fear, saying, "See, the humans have become like one of us, knowing good and evil, and now they might reach out their hands and take also from the tree of life and eat and live forever—therefore the Lord God sent them forth from the garden of Eden" (Genesis 3:22-23a).

Was expulsion from the garden a punishment? Perhaps. Currently my oldest child is a senior in high school. Every day is filled with discussion about hopeful plans, whispered laments of how things will be different, excitement about starting a new chapter, and regret over whether we've prepared her for adulthood. I'm not sure if it's the most appropriate reading of the garden story in Genesis 3, but as a parent of someone leaving the house, the story holds a new and nuanced meaning. It certainly seems like my oldest child has eaten from the tree of the knowledge of good and evil. At least, she thinks she has a well-defined knowledge of such ethical decisions. Looking back at my own story I can say that there is fear that she will be like "one of us," repeating the same blunders that I wished I had avoided. She won't be expelled from our home, but there will be a definitive difference between dependent and guest. Of course she will always be welcome in our home, but it will be different. She will be tilling and sowing and perhaps with a partner for the journey.

The story of the garden and my reflections on my child leaving home remind me that life's transitions are often marked by both loss and opportunity. Just as Adam and Eve's expulsion signaled a new way of relating to the world and to God, so does this shift in my family. Moving forward often requires letting go of what is comfortable and stepping into the unknown. It's a reminder that growth is seldom easy but is always necessary. This tension between staying and going, between comfort and challenge, is woven throughout Scripture, as God continually calls humanity to move forward into new chapters and new landscapes of faith.

God seems to want us to be on the move. From the beginning, we have resisted movement, resisted change, resisted the call to go where God is leading. But every time humanity tries to dig its heels in, God keeps nudging us forward. After Adam and Eve, Cain ran away from God by settling down in the land of Nod (Genesis 4:16). God removes the dry ground in Noah's day. Noah was called to drift on the sea while the earth swelled with floodwater. After hitting dry land he settled by planting a vineyard, and that story does not end well. It wasn't long before God's righteous Noah had too much wine and too little clothing (Genesis 9:20-21).

Then there's Babel—humanity's grand effort to settle in one place, to speak one language, to build a tower to the heavens. And God's response? God scatters them. Because the problem wasn't their collaboration; it was their sameness, their refusal to trust God's plan for diversity, and the audacious assumption that they could dictate where God was allowed and not allowed to be present. The Tower of Babel wasn't just a structure to be admired. It was a ziggurat, which is a building that is meant to house and confine a deity.

The journey of faith often carries with it a bittersweet mixture of obedience and hesitation. Like Abraham, we find ourselves torn between stepping into the unknown and clinging to the familiar. In our current political climate there is great uncertainty. Can you trust what those with power are promising, and if you can trust what they are saying, what does this mean for our future? To say "Do not be afraid" seems shortsighted, especially coming from me, a white, Southern, male clergyperson. I think there is great reason to be afraid. Hard-fought civil rights are disappearing, the class system is becoming a caste system in which those who are most vulnerable are being pushed further into the margins, affording the simplest of things has never seemed harder in our lifetime, and choices—from reproductive health, books on the library shelf, and posters on your child's elementary classroom wall—are fading. Saying "Do not be afraid" seems tone-deaf at best, but maybe Abraham's story, a perfect example of an imperfect faith, might guide us in understanding how to navigate the fearful uncertainty of tomorrow.

God calls Abraham to leave, and Abraham obeys . . . mostly. The story of Abraham's calling says that he went as the Lord had told him, and Lot went with him. Abraham was obedient, but he hedged his bets. He brought Lot along—a companion, a security blanket, a piece of the past, and I imagine God sighing. Abraham's decision to bring Lot with him, despite God's instruction, reflects a very human desire for security—a need to have a backup plan when faith feels too risky. Yet even in this act of partial obedience, God remains patient, walking with Abraham through his divided heart. This pattern of faith and hesitation reminds us that our journeys are rarely straightforward. Each step forward often requires a reckoning with what—or who—we are willing to leave behind.

Abraham reminds us that faith is often a tug-of-war between trust and control. We want to believe that God's promises are enough, but we also want to carry with us the familiar, the predictable, the things that feel like insurance against the unknown. God doesn't demand perfection from us—just the willingness to take the next step. Abraham's faltering faith didn't derail God's plan; it became part of the story. Perhaps that's the real miracle of faith—not that we get it right every time, but that God uses even our divided hearts to move us closer to the life we were created to live.

Moving forward in faith is never easy, especially when fear grips our hearts and uncertainty clouds the horizon. Where divisions run deep and anxieties about the future seem endless, it can feel almost impossible to trust in a plan we cannot fully see. Yet Abraham's story calls us to take those trembling steps forward, even when we long to cling to what feels safe and familiar. Faith is not about pretending fear doesn't exist; it's about choosing to believe that God's promises are bigger than our fears. Just as Abraham's hesitant obedience was met with God's patience, so too are we invited to trust that God is at work—even in the chaos, even in the unknown. The journey may feel daunting, but each step forward is a quiet rebellion against the pull of despair and a bold declaration that we trust the God who calls us to keep moving.

Abraham's story reveals that faith isn't linear. There's promise and doubt, affirmation and loss, and in the case of Abraham, Lot, and the Lord—bargaining. Was Lot supposed to accompany Abraham on his journey when the Lord said, "Go from your country and your kindred" (Genesis 12:1)? It almost seems that Lot was a kind of insurance policy. If

Abraham gets lost on the way to where God is showing him to go or if God doesn't keep the divine end of the bargain, Abraham has a fail-safe.

Have you ever kept an ace up your sleeve? Have you ever held back or held on just in case? As a clergyperson, I'd like to say it's complicated. I serve a congregation in an area of the country that is much more conservative than I am. I like to think that there is right, there is left, and there is gospel, but I can say with great confidence this is rarely how the good news is received. I mentioned from the pulpit one Sunday that "guns are not the problem, but our love of guns just might be." When the United States holds nearly half of the world's civilian firearms but only 4 percent of the world's population, that's a problem. I'm sure that 4 percent of a population having nearly 50 percent of anything is a problem. Mentioning this from the pulpit didn't go well. I was quickly dismissed by many as a liberal activist, which wasn't the insult those congregants thought it might be.

I felt God calling me into a "leave everything behind" moment to stand boldly against violence, but I bargained. I watered things down. I brought Lot with me, so to speak. There's a fine line between pastoral effectiveness, which always involves listening to diverse thoughts, and play-ing it safe because you know the cost. What I've learned is that the payment comes due anyway. I survived the day, but pandemics, disaffiliations, and tense elections that followed made things pretty clear that I was not compatible with many who had called my church home.

Abraham finally parts ways with Lot, and the loss is palpable. Relationships, like places, can tether us to what was, making it harder to embrace what is yet to come. As Abraham's story unfolds, we see that even the most faithful decisions come with a cost. Lot moves away toward Sodom, which complicates the story. The Lord reveals that Sodom is coming to an end, and Abraham bargains. Does this offer us permission to also barter with the divine? Is this a lack of faith or a faith that's stronger than anything I can muster?

Abraham's negotiation with God is fascinating because it reveals a relationship built on trust and honesty and a foundation that makes Abraham unafraid of tough questions. Abraham doesn't simply accept the decree without question but dares to advocate for mercy and questions God's justice. This moment suggests that faith isn't about blind obedience; it's about engaging with God in the complexity of life. Abraham's bargaining reflects a boldness that comes from knowing God's character—a God who listens, who is just, and who values righteousness even in the midst of judgment.

But what about us? Do we dare to approach God with such candor, bringing our fears, our doubts, and even our pleas for a different way? Like Abraham, we are often caught in the tension between God's call and the cost of following. We may find ourselves standing at a crossroads, negotiating with God, not out of defiance but out of a deep desire to align our hearts with God's will.

The bargaining I did with some of my congregants over my mention of gun violence certainly lacked Abraham's fervor. I see a similar thing in the church today. The language I was hearing leading up to several disaffiliation talks was something akin to "But we are traditional. Please don't leave," followed by a litany of time-honored creeds, John Wesley celebrations, and commitments to big tents. For good or ill, this didn't add up to much. It seems that both sides heard a lack of genuineness in the church's plea.

Perhaps the lesson here is that faithfulness is not a one-time decision but a series of choices—some marked by clarity, others by wrestling. And even when the cost feels unbearable, God remains present, inviting us into a dialogue that shapes us. What would it look like for us to embrace that kind of relational faith in our own journeys? Abraham wakes up one morning to see Sodom smoldering in the distance. Scripture never says that Abraham and Lot met again. For all Abraham knew, that chapter was closed.

I wonder if Abraham stood there in the aftermath, staring at the smoke, wondering what he could have done differently. Because here's the truth about faith: it doesn't promise a smooth path. There is always loss. There are always moments when we stand before God with empty hands and broken hearts. Faith requires us to let go—of comfort, of control, of the illusion that we are the authors of our own story. But here's what we know: God doesn't call us to movement without promise. God says to Abraham, *I will make you a blessing. Not your wealth, not your possessions, not your perfect life—you.* God takes Abraham's hesitations and missteps and transforms them into a legacy of faith.

This is the messy, holy paradox of faith: God works through our imperfections, our doubts, and even our resistance. Abraham's story reminds us that faith is less about arriving at a destination and more about continuing to walk, even when the way is unclear. But that walk often feels perilous, especially when those with power seem intent on marginalizing the vulnerable. It's no secret that throughout history—and even now—those in power have often wielded it not for justice but for self-preservation, creating systems that ostracize the very people God calls us to welcome.

The church, too, wrestles with this tension, don't we? Are we a people defined by radical hospitality, or do we cling to the security of safety? The same fear that led me to bargain with God's call also echoes in our institutions. It's the fear that if we let go of what we know, we'll lose everything. And yet, Abraham's story is a testament to what happens when we dare to release our grip on the familiar, even with imperfection. It doesn't mean the journey is without pain—Sodom burns, Lot seems lost, and Abraham stands in the ashes. But it does mean that God's promise persists, even in the aftermath.

In our personal wrestlings with faith, it's tempting to keep our aces tucked away, to hold back when the stakes are high. We fear the cost of speaking up, of standing boldly against injustice, of questioning systems that harm. Yet the gospel has always been at odds with the empires of this world. Jesus didn't tell us to stay safe; he told us to take up our cross. He stood with those on the margins—the poor, the outcast, the sinner—and called them beloved. And he calls us to do the same, even when it costs us.

Today, the stakes feel especially high. Political divisions deepen, and the church is often caught in the crossfire. There is fear—fear of saying the wrong thing, fear of losing people, fear of being labeled on one side, and the fear of being rejected, further ostracized or harmed, and diminished beyond viability on the other. The fear is real, even if the fears are experienced differently, with some holding higher stakes than others.

What would it look like for the church to fully embrace this call? To stop bargaining and start moving? It might mean losing members or resources. It might mean standing in the ashes of what was, like Abraham did, and wondering if we could have done things differently. But it also means trusting that God's promise holds—that even in our imperfection, even in our wrestling, God can and will bring blessing.

Faith calls us to movement, but movement always comes at a cost. Abraham's journey is not one of certainty but of courage. He walks forward not because he understands the full picture but because he trusts the God who does. And yet, his faith is not without flaw. He bargains, he hesitates, he clings to what is familiar—even when the familiar is no longer life-giving. Abraham's imperfect faith, like ours, is marked by moments of reluctance, doubt, and fear. But God doesn't abandon him. Instead, God transforms Abraham's faltering steps into the foundation of a covenant that spans generations.

The call to leave behind comforts—whether they are routines, relationships, or theologies—echoes in our own lives. Faith may mean standing in the tension of differing convictions without apology or bargain. It may mean losing what feels essential so that we can gain what is eternal. It may mean standing alongside those whom the world has cast aside or eating with Pharisees, which Jesus was known to do.

Faith over comfort. Faith over fear. This is not a call to recklessness but to trust—to believe that the God who calls us to movement is also the God who walks with us, who shapes us in the going, and who fulfills promises in ways we could never predict. Like Abraham, we may stand at the edge of the unknown, unsure of what lies ahead. But the promise remains: God is with us. And that promise, however imperfectly grasped, is enough to take the next step.

Chapter 2
Fearing
the Worst

Ann Atwater was an ordinary woman thrust into extraordinary circumstances. Living in Durham, North Carolina, during the civil rights era, she knew the ache of unfulfilled promises. As a single mother struggling to provide for her children, she clung to the hope that education could offer them a brighter future. When the Supreme Court handed down its landmark decision in *Brown v. Board of Education*, Ann believed that change was finally on the horizon. Equal access to education—it was a promise as bold as it was overdue.

But promises are rarely realized without struggle. In Durham, resistance to school desegregation was fierce, and progress seemed an impossibility. Ann quickly discovered that the road to justice was fraught with hostility, delays, and fear. Then came the invitation that would test her faith in the promise: she was asked to cochair a charette, a series of meetings with a diverse group of participants, to address school integration—alongside C. P. Ellis, a known leader of the Ku Klux Klan.

Imagine the tension of that moment: a Black woman committed to justice and a man whose very identity seemed to embody hatred and opposition. Ann could have walked away, citing the impossibility of collaboration. She could have chosen self-preservation, retreating to the relative safety of her community. And yet, she stayed. Guided by an unshakable belief in the dignity of every human being and the promise of equality, she faced her fears and stepped into what felt like an impossible task.

The meetings were grueling. Ann endured ridicule, threats, and frustration. C. P. Ellis was no less entrenched in his views, his presence a constant reminder of the animosity that permeated the community. But something remarkable happened. Through dialogue, persistence, and a willingness to see beyond the surface, Ann and C. P. began to find common ground. They both loved their children, and both wanted a better future. Slowly, barriers broke down, and their unlikely partnership became a catalyst for meaningful change in the Durham school system. Even more astonishing,

Ellis eventually renounced his Klan membership, a transformation born out of their shared humanity.

Ann Atwater's story is one of faith triumphing over fear. It would have been easy for her to focus on the threats, the hostility, and the impossibility of the task. Instead, she chose to trust in the larger promise of justice and equality. She refused to let fear dictate her actions, stepping into the unknown with courage and conviction.

God promised Abraham that he would become the father of a great nation, that his name would be revered, and that through him all the families of the earth would be blessed. Imagine the weight of such a promise—the divine assurance that one man's obedience would ripple across generations and nations. Abraham, faithful to God's call, packed for the journey ahead, carrying this monumental promise in his heart. As he traveled, his trust in God's plan was reinforced when God appeared before him at the oak of Moreh and declared, "To your offspring, I will give this land" (Genesis 12:7). It was a moment of clarity and affirmation, a glimpse of the promise taking shape.

With renewed purpose, Abraham moved on to the hill country, where he pitched his tent and built an altar to the Lord. This act of worship symbolized his trust in God's promise and his commitment to the journey ahead. Step by step, he ventured deeper into the unknown, journeying by stages toward the Negeb. Life seemed promising. The road ahead, though uncertain, appeared aligned with God's words. It felt as if everything was falling into place.

And then came the famine (Genesis 12:10). Wait...a famine? Just ten verses into this grand promise, and already there's talk of scarcity and hardship? This idyllic narrative is abruptly interrupted with a stark dose of reality, shattering the illusion of a smooth path to fulfillment. Perhaps this is a reality you know all too well. It's the moment when a promising beginning suddenly veers into unexpected difficulty, when hope begins to feel fragile and trust is tested.

It's like what I experienced as a freshman at LSU. My first-semester English professor was unusually laid back. From the very first day, it was clear that teaching was not his passion. He told us bluntly, "If you turn in your papers every two weeks, you don't need to attend the lectures." Naturally, I seized this opportunity, rarely setting foot in the classroom. It seemed too good to be true, but it worked—for a while.

Then came the spring semester. I scheduled my next English class at 7:30 in the morning, confident that LSU's English professors all followed the same low-key model. How wrong I was. My new professor was the opposite. Fresh out of graduate school, she approached her first teaching assignment with unrelenting enthusiasm and meticulous adherence to the syllabus. Attendance was mandatory and strictly enforced. Suddenly, what had felt like an easy road to success became a daily grind. To date, my grade for that semester remains one of the worst I've ever received.

Life has a way of challenging our expectations, doesn't it? Just when everything seems to be going smoothly, adversity steps in. For Abraham, the famine must have felt like an early betrayal of the promise. For us, these moments of disruption and difficulty often become defining points in our faith journey. Do we trust God's promises enough to persevere through the unexpected, through the famine seasons of our lives? Have you ever seen a promise melt away either through misplaced expectations or events beyond your control?

When my dad was in college, his dad, Big Bob, got really sick with pancreatitis. It wasn't long before he passed away, and it was a hard time for everyone. My dad decided he needed to drop out of school and go home to take care of his mom, Rita. It felt like the right thing to do. But when he showed up, Rita told him to turn right back around and get back to school. My dad has always been big on his faith. Growing up as a Missouri Synod Lutheran, he almost never missed a Sunday. He'd sit in the front row, singing hymns and chants at the top of his lungs. That connection to faith never wavered. Before I left for college, I asked him what I could do to build a strong faith foundation. So we sat down together and read through Romans. I also asked him why he never became a pastor, and he told me he had asked God about it once. God's answer? "I need you to be laity."

After Big Bob passed, my dad had a tough time with his faith. He was angry, and who wouldn't be? One night during prayer, he laid it all out: "I need to know if it's all true—the Bible, Jesus, everything—because I'm not going to ask again." Even though he was Lutheran, he had a moment that Wesley might've called his heart being "strangely warmed." That moment stuck with him. To this day, he's still singing in the front pew, living his faith in a way that's clear to anyone who knows him.

When Abraham faced famine, he fled to Egypt—a decision Scripture does not attribute to God's command. Did Abraham feel that the famine threatened God's promise, leading him to believe that moving to a place of abundance was the next right step? Or was he simply afraid—afraid he wouldn't have enough, afraid the journey would now be harder than he had anticipated? Perhaps his decision reflected a moment of doubt and self-preservation. It's difficult to say. Scripture rarely gives us the inner monologue we crave, leaving us to wrestle with questions that defy simple answers. Was Abraham's flight a faithful act of resourcefulness or a fearful detour from trust?

I'm not sure it's fair to declare one way or the other. Perhaps the nature of God's promises includes room for human improvisation—allowing for two steps back for every step forward as well as the winding, hesitant paths of discernment. After all, when Joseph fled to Egypt with Mary and the infant Jesus, he was warned in a dream. Abraham, however, received no such guidance.

Whatever we make of Abraham's decision, one thing is clear: it worked out for Abraham—but only for Abraham.

> *Now there was a famine in the land. So Abram went down to Egypt to reside there as an alien, for the famine was severe in the land. When he was about to enter Egypt, he said to his wife Sarai, "I know well that you are a woman beautiful in appearance; and when the Egyptians see you, they will say, 'This is his wife'; then they will kill me, but they will let you live. Say you are my sister, so that it may go well with me because of you, and that my life may be spared on your account." When Abram entered Egypt the Egyptians saw that the woman was very beautiful. When the officials of Pharaoh saw her, they praised her to Pharaoh. And the woman was taken into Pharaoh's house. And for her sake he dealt well with Abram; and he had sheep, oxen, male donkeys, male and female slaves, female donkeys, and camels. But the LORD afflicted Pharaoh and his house with great plagues because of Sarai, Abram's wife. So Pharaoh called Abram, and said, "What is this you have done to me? Why did you not tell me that she was your wife? Why did you say, 'She is my sister,' so that I took her for my wife? Now then, here is your wife; take her, and be gone." And Pharaoh gave his men orders concerning him; and they set him on the way, with his wife and all that he had.*
>
> *Genesis 12:10-20*

It took me far too long to notice Abraham's flight into Egypt—a story that, admittedly, rarely finds its way into sermons or Bible studies. It doesn't fit neatly into the image of "faithful Abraham" often shared and exemplified. But what happens when we pause to confront the uncomfortable realities embedded in this story? Abraham's actions in Egypt raise difficult questions about integrity and moral compromise. Could it be that his decision to present Sarah as his sister, exposing her to exploitation, places him among the ranks of biblical figures with seriously questionable judgment? Does this realization sit uncomfortably with our understanding of Abraham as a hero of faith? Perhaps it should. Should we extend grace to him, recognizing his human frailty, or should we wrestle with the tension his actions create in the biblical narrative? Saying that the Lord uses everyone regardless of ethical grounding is lazy theology. God does work with the unlikely and unlovable, but this isn't carte blanche for abusive and salacious behavior. Reconciling ancient stories with modern ethical sensibilities isn't easy, but it's necessary work. After all, our calling is to emulate Christ—not the flawed norms of any cultural moment, ancient or modern. In other words, we should imitate Christ, not the first century.

This tension cuts both ways. On one hand, it's dangerous to judge the actions of those in Scripture solely through the lens of today's ethical standards. Cultures and contexts shift, and understanding these shifts can illuminate the complexities of human behavior across time. On the other hand, it's equally risky to carry yesterday's assumptions into today as if growth and learning somehow undermine God's story. A deeper understanding of the world and the human condition doesn't threaten faith; it enriches it. God's truth is not a relic to be preserved but a living, breathing reality that unfolds in every generation. Growth isn't the enemy of tradition; it's the fulfillment of it, peeling back new layers of meaning and offering fresh insights into the beauty of God's story. Perhaps the real challenge lies in holding both truths together—the need to honor the past while remaining open to the Spirit's ongoing work in reshaping and renewing our understanding.

The story resonates with contemporary issues in profound ways. In a world grappling with systemic injustices, exploitation, and the misuse of power, Abraham's actions echo the ethical dilemmas we face today. Consider the stories in the news about human trafficking, abuse of power, and the commodification of human lives. These modern crises force us to confront the same fundamental questions: How do we respond when self-preservation conflicts with the well-being of others? What does it mean to live out our faith in the face of such moral complexities?

Take, for example, the recent controversies surrounding whistleblowers in corporate or governmental settings. In

2018 Christopher Wylie revealed how Cambridge Analytica had harvested the personal data of millions of Facebook users without their consent. This data was then used to create psychological profiles and influence voter behavior during major political events, including the 2016 US presidential election and the Brexit referendum.

Wylie faced significant risks in coming forward, including legal threats, professional ostracism, and personal attacks. Despite these challenges, he chose to expose the unethical practices he had witnessed, believing that the public had a right to know how their data was being misused. His revelations ignited global discussions about data privacy, ethics in technology, and the manipulation of democratic processes. Wylie's choice to speak out required courage and trust in the broader importance of transparency and accountability. His actions not only led to increased scrutiny of Big Tech but also prompted legislative changes, including the implementation of stricter regulations, like the General Data Protection Regulation (GDPR) in the European Union.

Regardless of scandal, individuals often face a stark choice: stay silent and preserve their careers or speak out and risk everything for the sake of truth and justice. Their stories are modern-day echoes of the tension in Abraham's narrative—a tension between fear and faith, between self-preservation and a higher calling. These parallels remind us that the ethical challenges of Scripture are not relics of the past; they are living realities that continue to shape our world.

The famine in Canaan was a test of Abraham's faith, one that revealed the fragility of human trust. Abraham fled to Egypt instead of staying in the land God had promised. This act of improvisation is deeply human, and it won't be the last time we hear of Abraham wanting to take matters into his own hands. Who among us hasn't struggled to trust God fully when faced with scarcity or uncertainty? And yet, Abraham's story challenges us to consider the consequences of our choices. His actions in Egypt may have ensured his survival, but they also caused harm to Sarah and disrupted the trust that should define a covenant relationship with God.

For some of us, the choice between self-preservation and sexual violence is more familiar than polite church-talk will allow. Sarah paid for Abraham's deception with her own body, and Abraham profited. It's important to acknowledge how deeply Abraham is flawed, and we must use this story as a means of moving toward solidarity with those who have been silenced.

The story of Sarah in Egypt is one that has troubled many readers, especially those who resonate deeply with her pain and perceived vulnerability. Her silence in Genesis 12 is unsettling, leaving her seemingly voiceless and passive. Yet ancient Jewish traditions, such as the Genesis Apocryphon, one of the Dead Sea Scrolls discovered in 1946 from Qumran, challenge this portrayal by reimagining Sarah not as a powerless victim but as a figure embodying profound wisdom and agency. These interpretations offer a compelling lens through which we can see Sarah's story anew—not as an erasure of her suffering but as a testament to her resilience and divine significance.

In the Genesis Apocryphon, Sarah is recast as a personification of Lady Wisdom, a recurring figure in Jewish wisdom traditions who represents divine insight, creativity, and the ability to navigate complex circumstances. Her wisdom, described as "great," and her presence likened to a date palm—a tree of life—elevates her role from silent object to active participant in God's unfolding story. This reimagination doesn't diminish the ethical tensions of Abraham's actions, but it does invite us to see Sarah's survival and influence as more than mere chance; it becomes an act of divine orchestration through her wisdom.

This portrayal resonates with the invitation of Proverbs to call wisdom your sister (Proverbs 7:4). For ancient storytellers, the identification of Sarah as Abraham's sister is not just a narrative convenience but a metaphorical alignment with the qualities of Lady Wisdom. Her so-called "ruse" before Pharaoh is reframed as a strategic exercise of wisdom, ensuring Abraham's safety while embodying the cunning often praised in biblical narratives. It's an interpretation that shifts the focus from Abraham's perceived failings to Sarah's strength—a strength rooted in her connection to divine wisdom.

These retellings don't erase the discomfort of the original narrative, and the Genesis Apocryphon also dismisses the suggestion that Sarah had intercourse with Pharaoh to "preserve" a priestly bloodline. Instead, they hold space for complexity. They remind us that God's faithfulness often unfolds in ways that challenge our ethical frameworks and stretch our understanding of justice. Sarah's story, as reimagined by ancient interpreters, becomes a bridge between her suffering and her agency—a reminder that even in her silence, her dignity was upheld by the divine.

For contemporary readers, especially those grappling with the implications of Sarah's abuse, these interpretations may offer a way to reconcile the discomfort of the text with the broader narrative of God's justice. They also serve as an invitation to consider how the stories of marginalized and silenced individuals can be reclaimed, not through denial of their pain but by amplifying their resilience and intrinsic worth.

In considering Abraham and Sarah's story, we might also reflect on the broader implications of faith over self-preservation in our own lives. What does it mean to trust God when the path ahead seems uncertain or even dangerous? How do we resist the temptation to prioritize our own safety and comfort over the well-being of others? It's a privileged position to even consider the question. Some don't have the choice. These are questions that demand not only introspection but also action. Faith is not a passive virtue; it's a dynamic force that calls us to live out God's promises in tangible ways.

Ann Atwater's story is one such example, but there are countless others. Consider the individuals who have risked their lives to protect refugees, the activists who have stood against systemic injustices, or the everyday people who have chosen kindness and generosity in the face of scarcity. These stories remind us that faith is not abstract; it's embodied. It's a choice we make every day to trust in God's provision and to align our actions with the divine vision for the world.

In the end, Abraham's escape into Egypt is not just about his failures; it's about God's patience and faithfulness toward humanity. It's a reminder that even in our moments of doubt and fear, God remains steadfast. God's promises endure because of grace, not perfection. This doesn't absolve us of responsibility; rather, it calls us to rise to the challenge of living out our faith with courage and integrity.

Faith often leads us into the tension of the unknown, demanding trust where certainty fails. Abraham sets out with God's word ringing in his ears, yet almost immediately, famine and fear cloud his vision. His decision to flee to Egypt is deeply human, a mix of pragmatism and doubt, courage and misstep. How often do we cling to control when God calls us to trust? How often do we prioritize safety over faithfulness, our plans over God's promises?

These ancient stories reverberate in our world today, where the tensions of faith and self-preservation play out in real and complex ways. What do I stand to lose by acting on faith and standing against the powers and principalities that are either silencing truth or dangerously re-narrating what goodness is. Faith over self-preservation is not a one-time decision. It is a posture, a way of moving through the world that consistently places trust in God's promises above our own fears and calculations. It calls us to stand with those who are vulnerable, even when it costs us something. It challenges us to speak the truth in love, even when silence might protect us. And it invites us to believe that God's vision for justice, reconciliation, and wholeness is worth it.

People are messy. Faith is not about perfect obedience or unshakable confidence. It is about returning to God, again and again, even when we falter. It is the paradox of faith: it demands everything from us, yet it does not depend on our perfection. In a world rife with ethical dilemmas, systemic injustices, and the temptation to prioritize self-preservation, these stories challenge us to ask, What does faith look like here and now? It may look like standing with marginalized communities. It may look like speaking truth to power, trusting that transparency is worth the risk. It may look like leaning in to the discomfort of hard conversations, like "What about Sarah, preacher?"

The promise God made to Abraham—to bless all nations through him—was never just about Abraham. It was a promise for the world, a covenant of reconciliation, healing, and hope. That promise continues today, calling us to participate in its fulfillment. It calls us to trust God's vision for the world, even when it feels distant or impossible. It calls us to act with courage and compassion, even when the cost is high. And it calls us to believe that, in the tension between fear and faith, God is always at work, weaving our stories into the greater story of redemption.

Ultimately, faith is not about the absence of fear but about the presence of trust. It is about believing that God's promises are true, even when famine looms and fear threatens to consume us. It is about stepping into the unknown, not with certainty, but with courage. And it is about choosing to live as though God's vision for justice, love, and reconciliation is not just a future hope but a present reality—one we are called to embody, here and now.

In the end, Ann Atwater and C. P. Ellis, Abraham, and even we are participants in the same story: a story of flawed people, faithful God, and a world in desperate need of both. And as we live into that story, may we, too, find the courage to trust God's promises, the strength to step beyond self-preservation, and the hope to believe that God's vision for the world is worth everything.

CHAPTER 3
WAITING ON THE PROMISE

I've always loved dad jokes. My parents tell me that my first joke was "Why did the elephant eat pisghetti?" The answer? "With its nose." One of my daughters had a favorite joke when she was little. It went like this:

> Knock, knock.
> Who's there?
> Banana.
> Banana who?
> Banana in ya face!

These jokes don't make sense, and they don't have to. Their charm lies in their simplicity, their absurdity, and the sheer joy they bring despite their lack of logical coherence.

Ambiguity doesn't diminish the laughter; it fuels it. It's a reminder that not everything has to be fully understood to be enjoyed.

My favorite kind of comedy is when the language is clever, full of innuendo, double entendre, puns, and unexpected turns. Around middle school I was introduced to Abbott and Costello's "Who's on First." It is a masterpiece of fast-paced, purposeful misdirection that takes the audience a moment to figure out what's going on. The same holds true with some of the great Monty Python sketches from their original BBC program. A classic sketch introduces a man who finds a clinic in which he can pay to have an argument. He enters a room and pays his cash to the man behind the desk. The man asks what he wants, with the customer replying that he's paid to have an argument. The man behind the desk says, "No you haven't." The customer answers back with, "Yes I have." The professional quickly says, "No you haven't," and so on. The man realizes that he's now in the argument that he's paid for, but the conversation enters a back-and-forth between yes and no. The customer protests, saying that what's transpiring isn't an argument, but a series of negations, to which the employee retorts, "No it isn't."

Part philosophical exploration and part verbal slapstick, moments like these bring about laughter and pondering. Ambiguity and laughter are also the threads that hold the middle of Abraham and Sarah's saga together, but it's not a comedy. Moments like these—part verbal slapstick, part intellectual exploration—invite both laughter and pondering. They show that ambiguity can be a powerful tool, offering layers of meaning that reward deeper engagement. This interplay of humor and uncertainty threads through the story of Abraham and Sarah, but it's not a comedy.

Abraham fell on his face and laughed, and said to himself, "Can a child be born to a man who is a hundred years old? Can Sarah, who is ninety years old, bear a child?" And Abraham said to God, "O that Ishmael might live in your sight!" (Genesis 17:16-18).

Abraham's laughter here feels nervous, almost involuntary—the kind of laughter that emerges when faced with the absurdity of the impossible. It's not the laughter of joy or delight; it's a reflexive response to something that strains the boundaries of belief. Maybe I'm projecting my own tendencies here, but I recognize that kind of laughter. It's the laughter that fills the silence when I'm unsure of how my words or ideas will land, a nervous chuckle to soften the edges of my uncertainty. But laughter isn't always a mask. Sometimes, it's the only way to grapple with profound truths. It becomes a subversive vehicle for revelation, breaking down barriers and inviting us to see the world differently.

There are four ways we share stories, especially in the face of imbalances of power, and each method shapes the kind of laughter or understanding it provokes. These modes of communication—public discourse, private conversation, disguised storytelling, and defiant declaration—provide a framework for understanding how we engage with truths that challenge us.

The first mode is public discourse, the kind of communication that occurs in the open for all to hear. Public discourse often operates within rigid structures. Consider a State of the Union address. The president highlights achievements while the opposing party delivers a rebuttal. The language is polished, predictable, and rarely disruptive. The goal isn't honesty in its purest form but clarity and safety. Public discourse is designed to maintain order, even when it gestures toward change.

In Abraham's story, we see elements of public discourse in God's covenantal promises. God's words to Abraham are grand and declarative: "I will make of you a great nation" (Genesis 12:2). The promise is bold and public, setting the stage for what is to come. But Abraham's laughter introduces a crack in the polished veneer. It's a private response to a public declaration, revealing the tension between the divine promise and human doubt.

The second mode is private conversation, a space where honesty often feels safer. These are the words spoken when the cameras are off or the meeting has ended. Private conversations allow for vulnerability, but when exposed to the public, they can provoke laughter or discomfort. Think of a hot mic moment—a politician caught expressing unfiltered thoughts. The laughter such moments evoke often comes from the shock of hearing something unscripted in a highly scripted world.

Abraham's private laughter and his plea, in Genesis 17:18, for Ishmael to live ("O that Ishmael might live in your sight!") show the vulnerability of a man wrestling with doubt. It's an intimate moment where his fears and desires spill out. This private discourse contrasts sharply with God's unwavering public promise, highlighting the tension between human frailty and divine faithfulness.

The third mode is disguise—stories that carry hidden truths beneath their surface. Disguised storytelling often emerges in oppressive contexts, where speaking truth directly is dangerous. Consider the tales of Br'er Rabbit, where the clever rabbit outwits more powerful foes. These stories, born out of the African American slave experience, were subversive commentaries on resistance and survival. The surface humor masked deeper truths about power and injustice.

Many of Jesus's parables function in this way. The story of the good Samaritan (Luke 10:25-37) is about neighborly love, but it's also a sharp critique of social and religious boundaries. Similarly, the healing of the ten lepers (Luke 17:11-19) celebrates gratitude but also challenges the audience's assumptions about who is worthy of God's grace. Disguised truths invite listeners to wrestle with deeper meanings, much like Abraham's laughter invites us to grapple with the audacity of God's promise.

Finally, there is defiance, the bold and public rejection of norms or power structures. Defiance is risky, often provoking strong reactions. When Jesus called the Pharisees "whitewashed tombs" (Matthew 23:27), it was a direct challenge to their authority. Defiance strips away pretense, forcing a confrontation with uncomfortable truths.

In Abraham's story, defiance appears subtly. His laughter and his plea for Ishmael could be seen as acts of resistance—a way of questioning God's plan. Yet even in his defiance, Abraham remains in conversation with God. This tension between questioning and faith is where transformation begins.

Laughter, whether nervous, joyful, or subversive, has a unique power to disarm and reveal. It's a spoonful of sugar that helps us swallow hard truths, but it's also a mirror, reflecting our doubts and hopes. Abraham's laughter reminds us that faith isn't always about certainty. Sometimes, it's about staying in the conversation, even when the promise feels impossible.

The story of Abraham and Sarah invites us to embrace ambiguity and tension not as obstacles to faith but as integral parts of the journey. It's in the spaces between laughter and doubt, promise and resistance that we encounter the divine. And like a well-told joke or a cleverly disguised story, these moments linger with us, inviting us to see the world—and God—in new ways.

I'm often asked, How do you know if you're following God's will? I feel that God has called me to be a pastor, but does that mean God specifically ordained me to write the book you're reading now? How detailed are God's plans for us, individually and collectively? It's a profound question, and I don't think there's a definitive answer. At times in Scripture, we hear God speak with absolute clarity through prophets. Other times, it seems God is surprised by how events unfold. Yet we can be certain that God does have a plan for us. We are called to do justice, love kindness, and walk humbly with our God (Micah 6:8). Through Christ, we learn to love God and love our neighbor. God equips us with gifts to serve one another and further the kingdom.

When God says, "I know the plans I have for you" in Jeremiah 29:11, God is speaking to Israel, the people of God—the "you" is plural. Just as some are teachers, others prophets or pastors (Ephesians 4:11), I don't think God's plans are so specific that God dictates every detail of our work. That responsibility is ours.

Our relationship with God and one another helps us discern our calling. Early in Abraham's story, the covenant is somewhat vague. But as we follow Abraham's journey, it's remarkable to see how God's promise grows in specificity, aligning with Abraham's shifting assumptions. When God promises Abraham that he will be the father of a great nation, Abraham seems to assume that his nephew, Lot, might play a role in fulfilling that promise. Abraham and Lot prospered together, so much so that they had to part ways to sustain their holdings. After Lot's departure, God speaks again to Abraham, perhaps knowing that Abraham had assumed the promise would be realized through Lot.

Sometimes, God speaks to us in ways that challenge our assumptions. Recently, I had an enlightening conversation with a dear friend of mine who is a pastor for a college ministry and a black, gay man. I asked him about his thoughts on the upcoming presidential administration and the election. He surprised me by saying, "I'll wait two years to weigh in." I was taken aback. Shouldn't he be anxious, joining the chorus of voices on social media demanding justice? Why wasn't he as alarmed as I was?

He explained, "As a gay, black man, no one in the Oval Office has ever truly advocated for me, so this is nothing new. My community is accustomed to those in power abusing their privilege without concern for minorities who can't sway the polls. For my own peace, I'm staying silent for at least two years." Many of my African American brothers and sisters resonate with this sentiment.

I had assumed his frustration mirrored mine, but I realized that God was speaking through him, challenging me to examine how deeply I had become entangled in my own story. As a white, Southern, left-of-center preacher, I've enjoyed certain privileges. Could it be that for the first time, I'm not getting my way—and that's what frightens me?

God visits Abraham again, reaffirming that his reward will be great. Abraham, now understanding that Lot is not the fulfillment of the promise, asks God, "What will you give me, for I continue childless, and the heir of my house is Eliezer of Damascus? . . . You have given me no offspring, so a slave born in my house is to be my heir." God responds with more specificity: "This man shall not be your heir; no one but your very own issue shall be your heir."

God then takes Abraham outside and says, "Look toward heaven and count the stars, if you are able to count them.... So shall your descendants be." Abraham believed, and the Lord counted this as righteousness (Genesis 15:3-6).

Abraham still has doubts. Though God has given him answers, he remains troubled by the lack of children of his own. The very next chapter begins: "Now Sarai, Abram's wife, bore him no children." As with the famine, God's promise is immediately challenged, and this covenant-burdened family is faced with a decision. Much like the famine inspired Abraham to flee either out of fear, self-preservation, or an honest attempt at saving God's preferred future, now Sarah is barren and maybe there is a need to improvise. Sarah encourages Abraham to conceive a child with her Egyptian slave, Hagar. Let us not miss that giving oneself to Egypt for the sake of taking control of God's promise is a recurring theme. During the Exodus ahead, there will be a constant temptation to return to Pharaoh.

I used to be confused, maybe naive, as to why so many in the pews and pulpits elect leaders whose campaigns are full of such destructive discourse, empty promises, and the apparent movement of wealth to those at the top of the economic leader—things that seem to be so counter to the gospel message. It goes beyond the tired "God can use anyone." That's only said when it's your preferred person in the White House. Regardless of partisanship, we like to take the role of Samuel, anointing God's chosen, assuming that the king will solve our problems. More directly, in Egypt you will do what you can to make sure you're holding the whip while another makes bricks. When a promise seems delayed, people will grab at it by any means necessary. We know how we treat those without power, which is why we are scared to death to lose it. At the suggestion to take Hagar, Abraham is obedient to Sarah without hesitation.

After Sarah offers Hagar, Abraham fails to mention that he's heard from God more than once and that he and Sarah would be conceiving a child for the future promise. Abraham is conveniently silent. The saga's narrator suggests that perhaps Sarah doesn't know of Abraham's divine discussions. As a result, Sarah offers Egypt just as she was once offered to it. It's complicated, cyclical, and full of lament.

When Ishmael is born, Hagar looks at Sarah with contempt. Sarah is angry and asks Abraham to do something about it. He responds, "Your slave is in your power; do to her as you please" (Genesis 16:6). The absurdity of this exchange reveals Abraham's passivity. Sarah is cruel, and Hagar flees. Yet the story takes a turn toward beauty when God calls Hagar to return and promises that Ishmael will be a free man, "a wild ass of a man." To our ears, this sounds harsh, but it means he will be free. Through Hagar, the cycle of slavery will be broken.

And then, Hagar names God. She is the first person in Scripture to do so, calling God El-roi—"the God who sees me." This moment is both beautiful and messy, complex and redemptive. Who do you see daily? Who sees you? Do you know what it's like to feel like you're not seen? As a tall, relatively menacing-looking person, I can't say that I've ever felt invisible. Not physically, anyway. Several years ago, I presented my first book, *The Faith of a Mockingbird*, at a forum at Myers Park United Methodist Church in Charlotte. After the discussion, a Black woman approached me and asked why I still made Atticus Finch the hero. I stupidly replied that he was the hero, completely missing what she was asking. Neither had I seen her in this moment, nor "seen her" in my writing. She said that I never mentioned Tom Robinson's wife. I was struck dumb. She said, "I'm not asking you to be a Black woman or to write as a Black woman, but I am asking you to make room for my story."

In such a complicated and messy saga, it's profound that the story uncharacteristically stops and makes room for Hagar. There are layers of lament and despair amid the closeness of God and God's promises of a great nation. A tradition suggests that after Sarah's death, Abraham marries Hagar, now known by her free name, Keturah (Genesis 25:1). I don't know if this is meant to be happy ending, empowerment, solidarity, or if the tradition is worth pondering. What we do know, depending somewhat on how we read the text, is that Hagar's descendants, the Ishmaelites, bring Joseph into Egypt near the end of Genesis. Sarah was offered to Egypt. Egypt was offered to Abraham. Their descendants are offered to Egypt, and the story continues. Egypt isn't the villain, but its function in the narrative tends toward that direction.

God goes to Abraham again and reminds him of the covenant, and Abraham falls on his face. God then adds some clarity. Sarah is also part of this promise, and this causes Abraham to laugh. "Can a child be born to a man who is a hundred years old? Can Sarah, who is ninety years old, bear a child?" And Abraham says to God, "O that Ishmael might live in your sight!" (Genesis 17:17-18). Understand that this isn't compassion being offered to Ishmael. If the promise can be through Ishmael, then Abraham never has to mention to Sarah God's persistent promising. Abraham doesn't have to face his own demons in pretending that Sarah was his sister or alluding to the necessity for Abraham to sleep with Hagar or the sin of saying that Sarah can do whatever she wants with Hagar if Ishmael is the promise. Abraham won't have to say anything, and everything will be fine.

In Genesis 18 Abraham is sitting by the entrance of his tent near the oaks of Mamre. When he looks up, he sees three men standing nearby. Without hesitation, Abraham runs to meet them, bowing low and offering his hospitality. "If I have found favor with you," he says, "don't pass by. Let me bring you water to wash your feet and bread to refresh you before you continue your journey."

The visitors agree, and Abraham springs into action. He rushes into the tent, instructing Sarah to knead and bake cakes from choice flour. He selects a tender calf from his herd, gives it to a servant for preparation, and gathers curds, milk, and the freshly prepared meat. With these offerings, Abraham serves the guests under the shade of the tree, standing by as they eat. This moment is rich with themes of hospitality, humility, and divine encounter, as Abraham's actions reflect both his reverence for others and eagerness to serve.

> *They said to him, "Where is your wife Sarah?" And he said, "There, in the tent." Then one said, "I will surely return to you in due season, and your wife Sarah shall have a son." And Sarah was listening at the tent entrance behind him. Now Abraham and Sarah were old, advanced in age; it had ceased to be with Sarah after the manner of women. So Sarah laughed to herself, saying, "After I have grown old, and my husband is old, shall I be fruitful?" The LORD said to Abraham, 'Why did Sarah laugh, and say, "Shall I indeed bear a child, now that I am old?" Is anything too wonderful for the LORD? At the set time I will return to you, in due season, and Sarah shall have a son." But Sarah denied, saying, "I did not laugh," for she was afraid. He said, "Oh yes, you did laugh."*
>
> *Genesis 18:9–15*

"Where is your wife Sarah?" It's a question Abraham's heard before, when he pretended that she was his sister. It's a question that we've heard before if we've been paying attention. Adam, where are you? Why are you hiding? Cain, where is your brother, his blood is crying to me from the ground. Abraham, where is your wife? She's there, in the tent.

One of the visitors says, "I will surely return to you in due season, and your wife Sarah shall have a son." Sarah hears this and laughs, just as Abraham had laughed earlier in the story. Then the Lord said to Abraham, "Why did Sarah laugh?" Abraham, why does Sarah not know? Why have you been keeping this promise to yourself? Is anything too wonderful for God?

Sarah, seemingly sensing the tension, denies that she laughed, to which someone says, "Yes, you did." Understand this isn't chastising Sarah. This is saying, "It's OK to be honest. You did laugh, and that's OK, because this isn't on you." Abraham has been trying to force an ending to the story. In hearing that he will have many offspring, he takes Lot with him. After Abraham and Lot part ways Abraham assumes and recommends Eliezer to be his heir. The Lord again announced the promise of progeny, and Abraham offers Ishmael. There is such lingering ambiguity, intrigue, messiness, and unknown, an under-the-surface, implicit battle between God's promise and the convenience of Egypt.

Laughter lingers, doesn't it? And it has many uses and meanings. It can veil our fears, soften our denials, or fill the space where words fail us. It can shatter pretensions, disarm offense, or bring absurdity to the surface. Sarah laughed in the tent, Abraham laughed in the open, and maybe somewhere, God laughed too—not in mockery but in the divine delight of possibility breaking through impossibility. Each laugh echoes something deeper, a reminder that in the strange intersection of faith and fear, promise and doubt, we find ourselves drawn closer to God.

The absurdity of Abraham and Sarah's story mirrors our own journeys. How often do we laugh—not in joy, but in disbelief—when faced with the enormity of what God calls us to? How often do we cling to the safe, the known, the "good enough," rather than stepping into the wilderness of God's promises? It's easier to settle for Egypt, to make peace with the present, than to hold out for a promise that stretches us beyond ourselves. Abraham's laughter was an attempt to contain the mystery, Sarah's an effort to mask the fear. And yet, both were drawn into the unfolding narrative of God's redemptive plan, a plan that did not hinge on their perfection but on God's persistent grace.

We like to control the narrative, to know where it's going, to have a say in the ending. But faith invites us into the tension of ambiguity. It's not about forcing a resolution but staying present, in the unresolved. Abraham's attempts to steer the promise—to make it fit his assumptions—are painfully familiar. Lot, Eliezer, Ishmael—each is a shortcut to avoid the vulnerability of trust. Yet God stays in the conversation, gently redirecting, revealing, and reminding: *It's not on you, Abraham. I am the author of this story*.

And what of us? Are we willing to step out from the tent, to risk the laughter of others as we claim the promises of God? Are we bold enough to hold the tension of waiting, to wrestle with the discomfort of uncertainty, to trust that God's plans are better than our shortcuts? Faith doesn't erase the messiness. It doesn't demand perfect belief, but it does call us to remain in the story, even when the ending feels impossible.

So laugh, if you must. Laugh at the absurdity of grace, the audacity of hope, the wildness of a God who sees us even in our hiding. Laugh not because you've figured it all out but because in the spaces of uncertainty and tension, God is already there, weaving together a story more beautiful, more redemptive, and more surprising than we could ever imagine. It's OK to laugh. It's OK to doubt. Just don't leave the conversation. Because that's where God does the most extraordinary work—in the messy, unresolved, tension-filled spaces of our lives. The promise is still unfolding. And the best stories always linger.

CHAPTER 4
THE ULTIMATE TEST

After these things God tested Abraham.
Genesis 22:1

One of the most striking moments in *The Lord of the Rings: The Fellowship of the Ring* takes place deep within the mines of Moria. The Fellowship, nine companions tasked with destroying the One Ring in the fires of Mount Doom to vanquish evil, has lost its way. They sense they are being followed. It's Gollum—the tortured creature who once possessed the ring—trailing them relentlessly, driven by an obsessive desire to reclaim it. Gollum's story is tangled with Bilbo's, the hobbit who took the ring from him, whether by clever chance or rightful contest, depending on whose version you trust. Now Frodo, the current ring bearer, finds himself in conversation with Gandalf, the wise and steadfast guide of their journey.

Frodo struggles with the burden of the ring, lamenting that it ever came into his life. He wonders aloud why Bilbo didn't rid them of Gollum when he had the chance. Gandalf, however, gently reminds him that it was mercy—pity—that stayed Bilbo's hand. The wizard points out a hard truth: the power to decide who deserves life or death lies far beyond human wisdom. Even the wisest cannot foresee the end of all things, and Gandalf muses that Gollum, broken and desperate as he is, may yet have a role to play in the story, for good or ill.

Frodo's despair echoes the hearts of many who find themselves caught in a liminal space, wishing that high-stakes burdens had never come. But Gandalf offers a quiet reassurance, reminding him that none of us chooses the times in which we live. What matters is how we use the time given to us. Beyond the reach of evil, Gandalf hints, there are forces at work shaping their paths with purpose, and that is a hopeful thought.

Perhaps J. R. R. Tolkien, in setting this scene in Moria, offers a subtle nod to another story: Abraham and Isaac's journey up Mount Moriah. In both tales, the weight of choice, mercy, and trust in a greater plan are at the heart of the story. Tolkien seems to hint throughout his epic that wisdom and faith often lie not in knowing the end but in walking forward with courage and hope, trusting that even the smallest acts of mercy can shape the fate of many.

The binding of Isaac in Genesis 22 is a troubling story. Wrapped up into the drama are questions about faith, ethics, trauma, doubt and even God's own omniscience. At the end of the story God says, "Now I know that you fear God" (Genesis 22:12). What do you mean, now you know? I can imagine a frustrated Abraham saying that he's left family behind, said goodbye to Lot at the destruction of Sodom, and sent Hagar and Ishmael away into the desert not knowing if they made it. There has been promise, doubt, affirmation, and at the end of every relative conclusion, loss. What do you mean, "Now I know"?

What do we know? And perhaps more important, what did Abraham know? The story of Abraham and Isaac on Mount Moriah is unsettling and ambiguous, leaving readers with more questions than answers. God commands Abraham, the faithful patriarch, to sacrifice his beloved son Isaac on a distant mountaintop. This moment of divine testing is deeply troubling not only for its stark demand but also for the questions it raises about God's will, obedience, and the nature of faith. It feels like a blanket that is just a bit too small. The more you pull at it, the more resigned you become to accept that it's just not going to cover everything.

This story doesn't offer easy answers. It unfolds like a dramatic ballet, with deliberate movements—plié down left, relevé, and lift—but the dancers' inner dialogue remains a mystery. Abraham's thoughts are hidden from us; Isaac's perspective is shrouded in silence; and God speaks only in commands. Yet through a patient and attentive reading, the silent steps of this narrative come together to reveal something profound and perhaps beautiful. But beauty, in this case, does not come without tension. The dance between Abraham, Isaac, and God seems to upend ethics and suspend any straightforward sense of moral law.

Some argue that whatever God commands is inherently good. If God ordains it, it must be right, even if it defies human understanding. This perspective, rooted in divine sovereignty, suggests that Abraham's unflinching obedience is the ultimate measure of faithfulness. But is it truly blind obedience that God desires? Or does the story invite us into a more complex engagement with faith and morality?

Sometimes when we think about goodness, we equate it with how something makes us feel or how effective it is. We might describe a thing as good because it produces happiness or because it works well. But goodness isn't confined to pleasant feelings or success. For instance, I can appreciate a good buffalo wing sauce when I taste one, but I'd struggle to make any moral claims about it. Similarly, medicine can heal, lower a fever, and sharpen the mind, yet ask a toddler about the goodness of antibiotics, and you're likely to get a very different answer.

This binding of Issac, and Abraham's story in general, seems to suggest that through grace, we are invited into discernment—into a kind of divine partnership where our understanding and agency matter, that faith is not submission but an ongoing dialogue with God. When Abraham learns of God's intent to destroy Sodom, he stands before the Creator of the universe and bargains, asking if God would wipe away the righteous along with the wicked. Perhaps if there are fifty righteous, God might see the error of divine ways and stay destruction. Abraham demonstrates that faith does not exclude reasoning, questioning, or even wrestling with God.

Are we so bold to look up to the heavens and ask questions that feel scandalously blasphemous? Abraham questions God's judgment, and although I may have thought in this way a time or two, I'm not sure I've ever vocalized my grievances with such conviction. Maybe you have. Maybe you've had moments when you've shaken your fists at the heavens in the darkness of reckless abandon. Maybe the trauma of loss in your story has been so great that you aren't sure if prayer is worth your breath. Maybe when Jesus mentions being forsaken on the cross it feels like Jesus is giving voice to your inner monologue you thought no one could understand.

There is precedent for Abraham to bargain with God, which doesn't make Isaac's binding any easier to understand. If Abraham questioned God before Sodom, why on Mount Moriah does Abraham not object to sacrificing his son? The silence is haunting, and it beckons us to fill in the gaps. Was Abraham so certain of God's faithfulness that he trusted there would be another way? I'm well aware that Hebrews 11:19 says that Abraham had considered that God would raise Isaac from the dead after the sacrifice, but the story from Genesis in no way suggests this. Scripture refers to itself in some outstanding and outlandish ways. Could it be that Abraham was paralyzed by the enormity of the moment? The text doesn't say, and perhaps that is its greatest challenge. It resists resolution, instead holding us in the tension between trust and doubt, obedience and agency.

This tension invites us into the story as participants rather than mere observers. It urges us to ask hard questions: What does it mean to trust God when divine will seems incomprehensible? Is faith about relinquishing all control, or does it involve active engagement with God's purposes? And when faced with what seems to be a moral paradox, how do we discern what is good and just?

Perhaps the story's power lies in its ambiguity, in the way it resists easy interpretation. It is a story that demands patience, humility, and a willingness to wrestle with the unknown. Again, like a ballet, its meaning emerges not in a single step but in the interplay of movement and stillness, sound and silence. Abraham's journey up the mountain, with Isaac carrying the wood for his own sacrifice, mirrors the steps of countless faith journeys—fraught with uncertainty, fear, and the hope that God will provide.

This dance of faith—of questioning, trusting, and discerning—is one we are all invited to join. It asks us to hold the tension between what we know and what we do not, to walk forward even when the way is unclear. And it challenges us to consider that the beauty of faith lies not in having all the answers but in trusting the One who leads the dance.

In 1635, Rembrandt offered a masterpiece interpreting the binding of Isaac, and I think it offers a picture of how we typically imagine this story. Abraham is overpowering Isaac, who is struggling to resist. Only Isaac's torso is highlighted, making him seem an impersonal sacrifice to a greater good. The knife appears to have been coming down as an angel swoops in at the last moment to stay Abraham's hand. This is why the first verse of this chapter is crucial. The narrator says "After these things, God tested Abraham" (Genesis 22:1).

We can argue over who is testing whom, but the story unfolds like that jarring interruption on the radio—the sudden, screeching tone followed by a calm voice reassuring us, "This is a test. This is only a test." The narrator of Genesis 22 wants us to know up front that this is not a story endorsing violence or child sacrifice. It is a test of Abraham's faith, not a command in the same sense as when God first called him: "Go from your country and your kindred and your father's house to the land that I will show you" (Genesis 12:1). The words in the two passages echo one another, intentionally drawing a parallel. Now, God commands, "Take your son, your only son Isaac, whom you love, and go to the land of Moriah and offer him there as a burnt offering on one of the mountains that I shall show you" (Genesis 22:2).

Go, Abraham. Leave behind your family again. Is this what God was asking all along? No, this is only a test. The narrator goes out of their way to let us know this. But what if it wasn't clear? What if Abraham's knife had moved too quickly, cutting short the angel's intervention? What if Abraham had never noticed the ram caught in the thicket? What if this entire story went tragically wrong? The narrator insists: no, this is only a test. There is no need to panic, to take shelter, or to draft your final will. The warning bells are ringing, but they're not heralding a real disaster. This is only a test.

Abraham's obedience is striking. Rising early the next morning, he sets out with Isaac and two servants, prepared to do what has been asked of him. When they arrive at the base of the mountain, he tells the two servants to stay behind with the donkey while he and Isaac go up to worship. Abraham tells them that they will come back, but what does Abraham really believe? Does he truly think that both he and Isaac will return? If so, can we call this faithfulness? If Abraham knows that God will intervene, is this test of faith genuine? It's almost like Jonah's resentment at the end of his story, when God forgives Nineveh. Jonah is furious, as if God's mercy is reckless and undermines his prophetic warnings. Could Abraham's calm confidence be a sign that he expects God to act mercifully—perhaps even recklessly? Or is he lying to protect Isaac from panic and escape?

Isaac's role is equally confounding. Strong enough to carry the wood for the sacrifice, surely Isaac is also strong enough to run from a man around a hundred years old. Did Isaac sense the gravity of what was happening? Was he complicit in some way, or did Abraham's words keep him from suspecting the truth? We don't know. We are left with unclear motivations, suspended and unresolved questions.

This narrative demands that we sit with uncertainty. While on the journey, Abraham and Isaac have their only recorded conversation in the Bible. Isaac calls out, "Father!" and again, Abraham responds, "Here I am" (Genesis 22:7). Then, the question hangs in the air, both simple and profound: "The fire and the wood are here, but where is the lamb for a burnt offering?" (Genesis 22:7). Abraham answers,

"God himself will provide the lamb for a burnt offering, my son" (Genesis 22:8). It's a statement full of ambiguity, inviting two unique interpretations. One reading suggests that Abraham believed God would ultimately intervene, that the sacrifice would not happen. "The Lord will provide the lamb, my son," is a word of comfort and providential peace. The other interpretation is more chilling. Abraham could be saying that God had provided Isaac as the sacrifice saying, "The Lord will provide the lamb—my son." Which interpretation is correct? Is that even the right question? We don't know, and perhaps we aren't supposed to.

When they reach the summit, the moment of decision arrives. Abraham binds Isaac's hands and feet, preparing to carry out the sacrifice. And then—intervention. God shows up. This is the moment Rembrandt captures in his famous painting, where an angel seems to descend in a rush, knocking the knife from Abraham's grasp. The divine voice breaks through: "Do not lay your hand on the boy or do anything to him; for now I know that you fear God, since you have not withheld your son, your only son, from me" (Genesis 22:12).

What are we to make of this moment? Some argue that this story exists to declare that God does not, or no longer does, require child sacrifice. Yet the historical and scriptural context complicates this claim. Consider Exodus 13:1-2:

"The LORD said to Moses 'Consecrate to me all the firstborn; whatever is the first to open the womb among the Israelites, of human beings and animals, is mine.'" Later in the Hebrew tradition, this command is euphemized to soften and relatively sanitize the seemingly clear meaning of the text so there is no tragic confusion.

Speaking of clear meaning, I wrestle with the idea that God tests us. Is divine trial theologically true? Perhaps, though I'm often left perplexed by what lesson I'm supposed to learn through purposefully inflicted hardship. It's one thing to coach your child through changing a tire. It's quite another to slash the tires when they're not looking. A loving God does not strike me as one who would sabotage just to see how we might respond. And yet, Scripture is full of tests— Abraham on Mount Moriah, Job in the ash heap, Jesus in the wilderness. But are these trials God's doing, or do they reveal something deeper about human nature, about the fragility of trust and the resilience of faith?

More practically, and possibly more troubling, is that the idea of divine testing often seems to be perpetuated by those who have survived hardship. This is not necessarily a means of celebrating God's offering of grace and perseverance but rather a veiled expression of pride—an unspoken hierarchy of spiritual toughness. I've heard it in testimonies, sometimes subtly, sometimes outright: *I was tested, and I passed.*

Look how faithful I am. Look how strong I've become. But where does that leave the ones whose hardship led not to triumph but to unraveling? What about the ones who didn't make it through unscathed? What of those whose loss has left them with a faith frayed at the edges, or worse, a faith that collapsed entirely?

And if we believe God is the one setting the hurdles, where does that leave grace? Where does that leave Jesus, who did not say, "Prove yourself worthy," but rather, "Come to me, all you who are weary"? (Matthew 11:28). If hardship is a test, then faith becomes a performance. And if faith is a performance, then we're left trying to impress the Creator of all things seen and unseen. But the gospel isn't a stage. It's an invitation, one that does not require us to earn our way through trials but to lean in to the presence of the One who walks through them with us.

The ambiguity of this story refuses to let us settle into easy answers. Faith, it seems, is not about clarity or certainty but about movement—stepping forward, even when the next step seems shrouded in mystery. It is about wrestling with questions that may not have answers and walking a path that often feels obscured. Abraham's journey invites us into this tension, urging us to ask, to struggle, and to trust that the story is still unfolding. There is more to see and hear as the journey continues, more to learn about the nature of God and the unfolding of God's purposes.

Then the men set out from there, and they looked towards Sodom; and Abraham went with them to set them on their way. The LORD said, "Shall I hide from Abraham what I am about to do, seeing that Abraham shall become a great and mighty nation, and all the nations of the earth shall be blessed in him? No, for I have chosen him, that he may charge his children and his household after him to keep the way of the LORD by doing righteousness and justice; so that the LORD may bring about for Abraham what he has promised him." Then the LORD said, "How great is the outcry against Sodom and Gomorrah and how very grave their sin! I must go down and see whether they have done altogether according to the outcry that has come to me; and if not, I will know."

So the men turned from there, and went towards Sodom, while Abraham remained standing before the LORD. Then Abraham came near and said, "Will you indeed sweep away the righteous with the wicked? Suppose there are fifty righteous within the city; will you then sweep away the place and not forgive it for the fifty righteous who are in it? Far be it from you to do such a thing, to slay the righteous with the wicked, so that the righteous fare as the wicked! Far be that from you! Shall not the Judge of all the earth do what is just?" And the LORD said, "If I find at Sodom fifty righteous in the city, I will forgive the whole place for their sake."

Genesis 18:16–26

Could it be that the real test, so to speak, was an invitation for Abraham to intervene when God commanded him to sacrifice his son? Maybe the test was never about whether Abraham would comply, but whether he would dare to push back—to say, *No. This isn't right. This isn't just.* After all, he had done it before. When God declared judgment on Sodom, Abraham stepped forward, interceding on behalf of the righteous. "Will you indeed sweep away the righteous with the wicked?" he asked. "Far be that from you! Shall not the Judge of all the earth do what is just?" He pleaded, bargained, argued for the lives of those he had never met. So why didn't he argue for his own son? Why did the Abraham who challenged God on behalf of strangers suddenly fall silent when the stakes became more personal?

Maybe this story reveals something else about human nature—about how we can become so preoccupied with pleasing God that we forget about the people right in front of us. Maybe the true crisis in this passage is not simply the demand for sacrifice but the single-mindedness with which Abraham moves toward it. The angel's intervention is the clue:

> *"Do not lay your hand on the boy or do anything to him, for now I know that you fear God, since you have not withheld your son, your only son, from me." And Abraham looked up and saw a ram, caught in a thicket by its horns. Abraham went and took the ram and offered it up as a burnt offering instead of his son.*

> *Genesis 22:12–13*

Notice what the text does not say. It does not say that a ram appeared in the thicket at that moment. It does not say that God provided it right then and there. It says that Abraham looked up and saw it. It sounds like the ram had been there the whole time, long enough for its horns to become tangled, long enough for it to have already been waiting.

How long had the ram been there? Long enough for Abraham to have noticed it earlier—if he had been looking. But he wasn't. He was so fixated on obedience, so convinced that this was the path God had set before him, that he didn't see the provision that had already been made. His eyes were on the altar, not on the alternative.

And that is the danger, isn't it? That obedience, unquestioned and unwavering, is what God most desires. But what if faithfulness isn't just about following orders? What if it's also about watching, listening, discerning, sometimes pushing back on behalf of the vulnerable? What if it's about knowing the character of God well enough to recognize when something doesn't line up, when we have misheard, misread, or misunderstood?

If you think following God means sacrificing your child, at the very least look up. There may be a ram caught in the thicket. If you think following God means walking headlong into suffering without question, take Abraham's lead in Sodom and argue, question, bargain, and put up a fight. Because sometimes faithfulness looks like asking better questions. Sometimes faithfulness looks like wrestling with God.

And sometimes faithfulness looks like stopping.

The Lord did indeed provide the Lamb. And when that Lamb finally spoke, when Jesus walked among us, he did call for sacrifice but in the context of love, mercy, and justice. Obedience to God does not mean blind compliance to what we think God is asking of us. It means aligning ourselves with God's heart and character. It means knowing that the One who stopped Abraham's hand is the same One who, centuries later, stood between a woman and her accusers asking who would be the first one to throw the stone of shame, the same One who healed on the Sabbath, the same One who fed thousands, welcomed the sinner, and touched the untouchable. It means understanding that the God who stayed Abraham's hand is not the kind of God who hopes you don't stumble over purposefully placed hurdles but the kind who steps up to carry a cross of redemption.

And so, if ever we find ourselves in a place where obedience seems to demand cruelty, where faithfulness seems to require the harm of another, where devotion leads us to justify destruction, we should stop and look up. We may be missing the ram in the thicket. We may be missing the grace that was always there, waiting to be seen.

This story is not simply about Abraham's obedience. It is about divine intervention. It is about the mercy of God interrupting the flawed faithfulness of people. That sounds like the gospel. The Lamb has been provided, my child. God does not stand apart, demanding that we justify ourselves but steps in, providing what we could not provide for ourselves. In Christ, we see the full and final revelation of who God is—a God who desires mercy over sacrifice.

Rembrandt sketched this scene a second time in 1655, twenty years after the first painting. His second offering is quite different from the first. Abraham looks grieved, covering a willing Isaac's eyes instead of forcefully pushing down his face. The angel doesn't swoop in; rather the angel is comforting Abraham, whose knife is passively upturned, held away from his son, in his nondominant hand. Art, in the same way as with Scripture, is open to interpretation. Maybe twenty years of living softened Rembrandt's understanding of what God was asking Abraham to do.

Faith is rarely clean. It does not unfold in a straight line, nor does it reward those who navigate it flawlessly. Abraham's journey was marked by hesitation, missteps, and uncertainty. He faltered in Egypt, wavered in Gerar, laughed at the impossibility of God's promise, and yet, he continued walking. His faith was not perfect, but it was persistent. And perhaps that is the truest kind of faith—not the kind that never questions, but the kind that keeps moving forward despite the questions.

The binding of Isaac is often framed as Abraham's ultimate test, but maybe it is better understood as a window into the tension of faith itself. Is faith about unquestioning obedience, or is it about seeing—truly seeing—the character of God? Abraham's silence on Mount Moria is deafening, especially when contrasted with his bold intercession for Sodom. Why did he not plead for his own son? Why did he not push back, argue, or ask the same questions he once asked on behalf of strangers? Was this faith, or was it fear?

And yet, even here, grace interrupts. The ram in the thicket had been there all along. The provision was not absent, only unnoticed. How often do we move through life convinced that faithfulness means walking alone, that God is watching but not intervening? How often do we cling to fear disguised as devotion, forgetting that God has already made a way?

Abraham's story is not about perfect faith, but about faith that keeps going—faith that learns, stumbles, and still reaches toward trust. His journey reminds us that faith is not the absence of fear, but the refusal to let fear have the final word. And sometimes, all it takes to break fear's grip is to stop, to look up—and to finally see.

CONCLUSION

Faith has always been a conversation more than a certainty, a journey more than a destination. Abraham's story reminds us that faith is rarely linear, bending and folding, sometimes yielding to fear, sometimes surging forward with reckless abandon. As we have walked through his story together, we've seen moments of brilliance and moments of hesitation, times of unquestioning obedience and moments of self-preserving calculation. Abraham is not a model of perfect faith but a faithful story that struggles, wavers, and sometimes stumbles forward more by grace than certainty.

Perhaps that is where we find ourselves most clearly in Abraham's story. Not in the grand moments of covenant or in the celestial promises that feel too vast to comprehend, but in the places where doubt creeps in, where fear whispers that we should turn back, where we take matters into our own hands because waiting seems unbearable. We know what it is to wrestle with faith, to wonder if God is truly leading, to question whether we heard correctly in the first place. And yet, like Abraham, we find that faith is not about having all the answers but about continuing the conversation with God.

Fear is not merely an ancient struggle but a persistent companion in our own unsettled times. It's foolish and misguided to simply say, "Don't be afraid." There's plenty to fear. Just as Abraham stood at the crossroads of trust and self-reliance, we too navigate a world marked by uncertainty—economic instability, political division, personal losses, and the gnawing question of what the future holds. The same whispers of doubt that urged Abraham to take control echo in our own anxieties, tempting us to seek quick solutions rather than wait in faith. Fear is the quiet, isolating lie that encourages scarcity, defeat, and the deprived imagination that assumes hope is impossible. And so, we keep moving to build altars and alternatives in the moments of clarity that sustain us through the unknown.

Abraham's story gives us permission to acknowledge that tension in our own journeys, to be honest about our fears without being consumed by them. If faith were a matter of certainty, Abraham would not have needed so many reassurances, so many altars built in moments of clarity before wandering again into uncertainty.

One of the most striking things about Abraham's journey is how often he improvises. We see him move forward when God calls, but we also see him react when fear grips him.

He leaves his home but brings Lot as an extra safety net. He believes God's promise but hedges his bets with Hagar. He trusts that God will provide, yet he also schemes in Egypt to protect himself. His story is full of these contradictions, and yet, if faith is anything, it is the willingness to keep showing up despite the contradictions.

Faith is a willingness to stay in the struggle—to wrestle, like Jacob at the riverbank, until we walk away changed, even if we walk with a limp. Faith is what allows us to keep walking even when the path ahead is obscured. It is what keeps us tethered to hope even when the evidence seems scarce. Faith, in its most honest form, is not about never being afraid, but it is about refusing to let fear have the final word.

Abraham's journey, like ours, is filled with waiting. Waiting for a child, waiting for a promise to take shape, waiting for clarity that never seems to arrive on our timetable. The waiting is difficult. It stretches us. It exposes our impatience and our need for control. And yet, God does not seem to be in a hurry, though at times I sure wish the Divine would speed things up. The long road to fulfillment is not a mistake—it is the very ground on which faith is formed. If faith was merely about outcomes, then the waiting would be unbearable. But if faith is about relationship, about trusting that God is with us in the in-between places, then waiting is not wasted time. It is sacred space where God's presence is made known.

Conclusion

It would be easy to make Abraham a hero, to polish his story into a narrative of unwavering trust. But Scripture does not give us that luxury. At least, it shouldn't. Instead, it gives us an Abraham who hesitates, who miscalculates, who sometimes acts out of fear rather than trust. So perhaps this is the takeaway: faith does not require perfection. It does not demand certainty. It does not ask that we never waver, never hesitate, never question. Faith, at its core, is simply the refusal to walk away. It is staying in the tension long enough to see that God is still at work, even in our doubt, even in our waiting, even in our failures.

As we conclude this exploration of Abraham's journey, the heart of the matter seems to rest not in a faith that never falters but in a faith that refuses to give up. Abraham's life teaches us that faith is rarely neat, never without its doubts, and often accompanied by a fair share of improvisation. The question is not whether we will face fear—it's inevitable—but whether we will allow it to determine our steps. Will fear define the edges of our faith, or will we press beyond its borders, daring to trust that God is present even in the unmarked spaces of our lives?

Abraham's story offers no guarantee of simplicity, no promise that the journey will be straightforward or that we will always choose well. What it offers instead is the assurance that God remains steadfast, even when we are unsteady. So as we find ourselves standing at our own crossroads—between trust and self-reliance, between fear and faith—what choices will we make?

The road is uncertain, but the promise remains: we are never left alone. Perhaps, in the end, that is the invitation—to walk this journey with open hands, trusting that the God who called Abraham still calls us, even in our doubts, even in our questions, even in our fear. Perseverance seems to be faith's legacy, the refusal to be defined by anything other than God's grace. And maybe that is enough.